The patterns in Pascal's Triangle offer a remarkable variety of opportunities for number work at many different levels. It is a rich resource and has many possible places to enter the curriculum and so a simple set of reproducible worksheets would be a limitation rather than an asset. The blackline masters included here are intended to be a starting point for teacher-designed worksheets adapted for a particular class on a particular occasion. The text of the book is devoted to advice and suggestions on how the material might be used in class or to point out possible lines of investigation.

CONTENTS

USING THE BLACKLINE MASTERS

Use the blackline masters by first making a single photocopy of the one required. Then modify it with black ink by adding a suitable title and the questions, suggestions or problems needed. From this "customised" master run off as many copies as required. Remember that you can always delete numbers or lines from the copy by using a white typewriter correcting fluid or by glueing white paper or a white label over portions you do not want.

Whatever the application or need, one or other of the masters should provide a suitable starting point. Some of the masters show the numbers of Pascal's Triangle placed into touching squares, and this method of presentation is useful for dealing with the addition properties. Other masters place the numbers in smaller squares, and this method of presentation is more suitable for investigations into the properties of rows, columns or diagonals. There are also outlines containing no numbers and numbers without outlines and so it is a case of choosing the most suitable one for the lesson you have in mind.

There are as many ways of introducing Pascal's Triangle as there are teachers and classes, but it is of great importance for us to keep in mind the excitement and the initial impact of meeting its remarkable properties for the first time. With this in mind it seems a great pity to simply hand out a master of a completed triangle.

Some teachers might prefer to start by handing out a triangular grid with a few numbers in it like the one here and then to ask the class first to deduce the rule which has been used and then to use this rule to continue the pattern further.

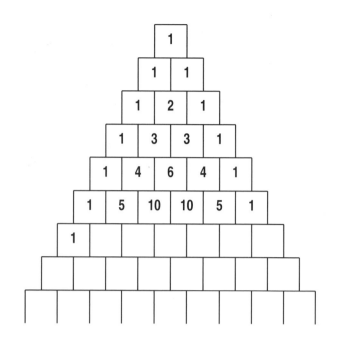

Others might prefer to supply a blank outline and to suggest that the class place a single 1 in the first square. If the outside of the triangle is considered to be entirely zeros, then the whole pattern can generated by applying the addition rule line by line.

ADDITION RULE

First row		1		
Second row	0+1=1		1+0=1	
Third row	0+1=1	1+1=2		1+0=1

Few children fail to respond to the fact that the triangle seems to grow from a single 1 appearing in a universe of zeros, even if they wouldn't express it like that!

After the initial introduction, it might be useful to reinforce knowledge about the addition rule by providing incomplete portions of the Triangle and treating them as puzzles. There is satisfaction for everyone in completing the blank squares of Masters 2 and 3 because after several lines of addition the answer should correspond to the printed figure. Don't forget that if you would like to use the outlines but wish to substitute your own numbers, then it is a simple matter to make a blank master by using typewriter correcting fluid.

Inventing new puzzles like these is a useful follow-up activity for the pupils also.

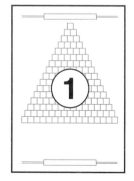
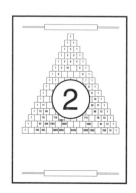
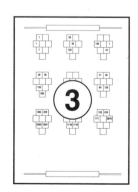

PASCAL'S TRIANGLE

A teacher's guide with blackline masters
Tony Colledge

```
                                    1
                                 1     1
                              1     2     1
                           1     3     3     1
                        1     4     6     4     1
                     1     5    10    10     5     1
                  1     6    15    20    15     6     1
               1     7    21    35    35    21     7     1
            1     8    28    56    70    56    28     8     1
         1     9    36    84   126   126    84    36     9     1
      1    10    45   120   210   252   210   120    45    10     1
   1    11    55   165   330   462   462   330   165    55    11     1
 1    12    66   220   495   792   924   792   495   220    66    12    1
 1   13   78   286   715  1287  1716  1716  1287  715   286   78   13   1
1   14   91   364  1001  2002  3003  3432  3003  2002  1001  364   91   14   1
1  15  105  455  1365 3003 5005 6435 6435 5005 3003 1365  455  105  15   1
```

"The pattern is so simple that a 10 year can write it down, yet it contains such inexhaustable riches and links with so many seemingly unrelated aspects of mathematics, that it is surely one of the most elegant number arrays."

Martin Gardner - Mathematical Carnival

TARQUIN PUBLICATIONS

BLAISE PASCAL (1623 - 1662)

In his short but eventful lifetime, the French mathematician and scientist worked on many different problems and topics. He invented a calculating machine, worked on the barometer and produced a treatise on conic sections.

The triangle which bears his name was known in China in around 1300 A.D. and probably in Europe also, but it was Pascal's extensive work on probability theory which caused it to be named after him. He also wrote a number of religious pamphlets and a book called "Pensées"(Thoughts).

This poster by Tony Colledge is in full colour and is available from Tarquin Publications, as are other mathematical books and materials. Please write to the address below for a catalogue.

© 2004   Tony Colledge
© 1992   First Edition
I.S.B.N.:   0 906212 84 7
Design : Magdalen Bear
Cover   : Gerry Downes
Printing : Fuller-Davies Ltd., Ipswich

Tarquin Publications
Stradbroke
Diss
Norfolk IP21 5JP
England

PAVING STONES

In a certain shopping precinct there are some white paving slabs set into the grey ones in a triangular pattern. The first one is marked with a star. If a child starts always on the marked square, what is the fewest number of steps he or she needs to take to reach each white slab? They are not allowed to jump over any row or to step off the white slabs.

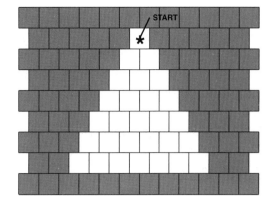

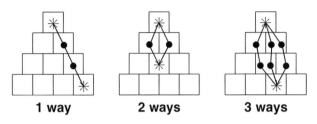

| 1 way | 2 ways | 3 ways |

It is likely that the investigation will start with a series of sketches like the ones above. It shows the different routes which could be taken to reach each of three particular squares. Sufficient time should be allowed for this activity so that it becomes absolutely clear that this is a manifestation of Pascal's Triangle.

ADDING THE ROWS

At a very early stage in the study of Pascal's Triangle, it is a good idea to ask the class to add together all the numbers in each row. As soon as the pattern of doubling is noted, it is best to make the suggestion that the totals should be expressed as powers of two.

$$2^1, \quad 2^2, \quad 2^3, \quad 2^4, \quad 2^5, \quad 2^6 \ldots$$

Since the indices are the counting numbers and they appear on the first diagonal, it is then appropriate to point out that

$$2^0 = 1$$

and therefore that it is the convention to number the rows 0, 1, 2, 3, 4,... and not 1, 2, 3, 4, as might seem to be natural at first sight.

The number of the row is therefore the counting number in the first diagonal.

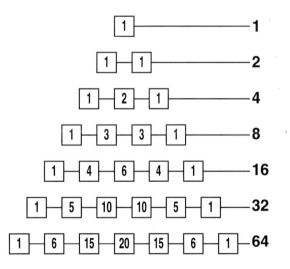

ALEX and HER BICYCLE

Alex was nearly 10 years old and her father asked her what she would like for her birthday. She would have liked a new bicycle, but instead of asking for some money towards it she said, "I would like £1 for every different way that I can find of adding whole numbers together to make my age". Her father was not a mathematician, and thought that there might be about 20 ways to find numbers which added up to 10. He agreed. How much did he have to pay?

This is a fine example of the type of investigative mathematics we want to encourage. Start by asking the class to solve it directly by listing all the possibilities.

Most pupils will begin with   **1 + 9, 2 + 8, 3 + 7,** etc.

and the question soon arises whether pairs of numbers like **1 + 9** count as being different from **9 + 1**. It is necessary to agree that they are different.

Should zeros be allowed? Say no. Fractions and decimals are excluded by the phrasing of the problem.

They soon realise that   **1 + 3 + 6** or **2 + 2 + 2 + 2 + 2**

or even   **1 + 1 + 1 + 1 + 1 + 1 + 1 + 1 + 1 + 1**
are also solutions.

After about 20 or 30 minutes, each of them may have a list of between 50 and 100 different combinations and that is probably the point to stop it. Can we not do the search in a more logical way and so be sure of not missing any? Would the problem not have been easier if she had been younger?

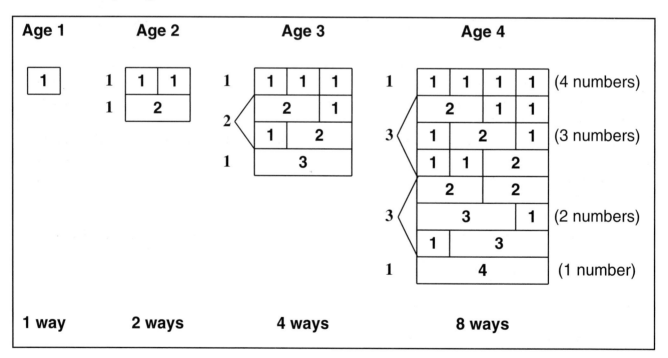

A diagram like the one above, worked out in a logical way, clearly shows the connection with Pascal's Triangle and that the sum of all the possibilities for each age is a power of two. It soon becomes apparent that for her 10th birthday she would get 2^9 or £512.

How much would she get on her 18th or 21st birthday?

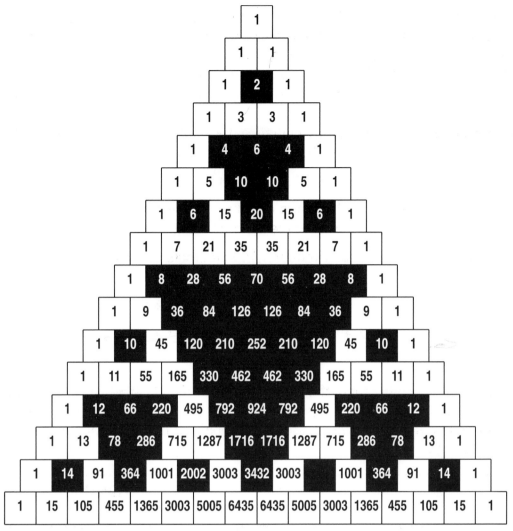

This diagram shows a blackline master 5 with all the squares which contain an even number coloured black. It immediately shows interesting patterns of stepped triangles of different sizes. The bases of those triangles are of sizes 1, 3 or 7 numbers. Continuing further, row 16 will be entirely even except for the two ones at each end and it will be the start of another triangle with its base 15 units long. Children will soon spot the rule of "double it and add one" and this may be another occasion to talk of indices. It is not difficult to deduce that row 32 must be the start of a new larger triangle with a base of 31 even numbers.

Since the rule for calculating each element of Pascal's Triangle is to add together the two adjacent numbers in the row above, this is a good opportunity to talk about the addition properties of odds and evens.

> **ODD + ODD = EVEN**
>
> **EVEN + ODD = ODD**
>
> **EVEN + EVEN = EVEN**

With these relationships in mind, it is easy to see why the pattern must consist of stepped triangles.

Generating the pattern made by colouring the multiples of other numbers is a natural extension of the work on odd and even numbers. Even with only 15 rows, the patterns generated by each number are easily recognisable. They are distinctly different, yet essentially similar! The class can be divided into groups, so that in a relatively short time it is possible to make a complete set of the patterns generated by all numbers up to 10, 11 or 12.

Multiples of 3

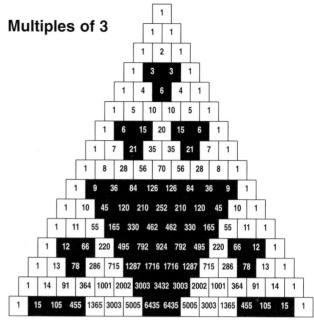

Multiples of 5

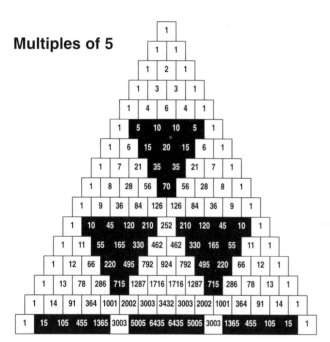

Multiples of 7

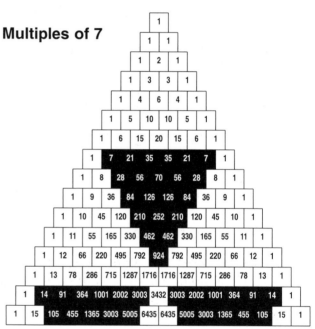

If it is decided to go further than this and to produce large wallchart-sized illustrations of some of the patterns, then the outlines can be created by first making several copies of blackline masters 6 and 7. These copies can be cut out and pasted together to give a collage with the required number of rows. Another possibility if you have access to a photocopier with an "enlarge" facility, is to use blackline master 8 as the starting point.

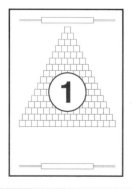
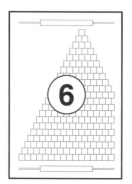
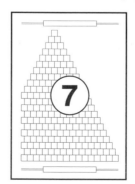

ODDS and EVENS

ROW		ODD	EVEN
0	1	1	0
1	1 1	2	0
2	1 2 1	2	1
3	1 3 3 1	4	0
4	1 4 6 4 1	2	3
5	1 5 10 10 5 1	4	2
6	1 6 15 20 15 6 1	4	3
7	1 7 21 35 35 21 7 1	8	0
8	1 8 28 56 70 56 28 8 1	2	7
9	1 9 36 84 126 126 84 36 9 1	4	6

It is interesting to speculate whether there are always more odd numbers than even in Pascal's Triangle, no matter how many rows it is continued for. Certainly the odd numbers outnumber the even in the early rows. However in row 8 the even numbers outnumber the odd by seven to two. Does this mean that the even numbers will eventually catch up?

It makes a useful investigation to ask the class to count the even and odd numbers in each row and then to produce accumulative totals and possibly graphs of their results.

With more able classes it is more interesting to encourage a search for a logical method of calculating the proportions of odd and even numbers. The diagram on page 7 will help because it shows that the even numbers form a pattern of triangles of different sizes.

It can also be seen that rows 3, 7, 15, 31 ... consist of only odd numbers and are therefore convenient stopping places in the counting process. At each of those rows all the triangles of even numbers above are complete and therefore counting the accumulative totals is made simpler.

Some triangles contain just 1 even number, some contain 3 + 2 +1 = 6 even numbers, some 7 + 6 + 5 + ... = 28 and so on. It is evident that row 16 will be the start of a larger triangle which contains 15 + 14 + 13 + ... = 120 even numbers. It must be completed in row 30, because row 31 is completely odd.

Teachers might care to pose the question in the form

"What is the ratio of even to odd numbers after 3, 7, 15, 31, 63, 127, ... rows?"

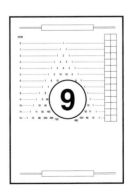

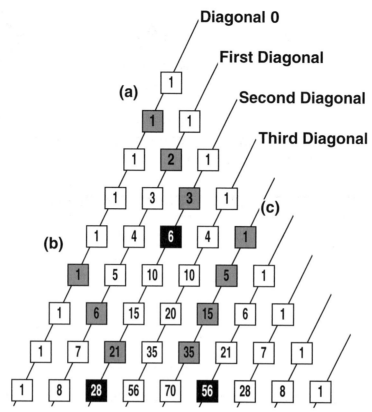

It is consistent to number the diagonals in a way similar to that used for the rows, calling the outer lines of 1s "diagonal 0". The next diagonal, which lists the counting numbers 1, 2, 3, ... is therefore called "diagonal 1" or "the first diagonal". This is convenient because it means that the counting number which is on the first diagonal gives the number of the row. The second diagonal lists the sequence of triangle numbers and adjacent pairs give the square numbers. The third diagonal gives the sequence of tetrahedral numbers and adjacent pairs give the pyramid numbers. Further investigations will find other properties of the diagonals.

Perfect Squares

The sum of any two adjacent numbers on the second diagonal is always a perfect square.

> 1 + 3 = 4
> 3 + 6 = 9
> 6 + 10 = 16
> 10 + 15 = 25
> .....

Edge Worms

The sum of the numbers on any diagonal starting at an edge is always equal to the next number on the other diagonal.

(a) 1 + 2 + 3 = 6

(b) 1 + 6 + 21 = 28

(c) 1 + 5 + 15 + 35 = 56

Is the sum ever equal to the next number on the same diagonal?

| 1 | 3 | 6 | 10 | 15 |

It is likely that many children will already have heard of triangle numbers and therefore already have noticed that they appear on the second diagonal. If not, then it is best to introduce them by means of a pattern like the one above.

NUMBER OF ROWS	TRIANGLE NUMBER
2	1
3	3
4	6
5	10
6	15

What is the rule for working out the triangular number on the second diagonal given its row number? Which triangle number comes into row 10, row 15, row 100 etc.?

INTERSECTING LINES

Investigate how many intersections are created by drawing certain numbers of straight lines.

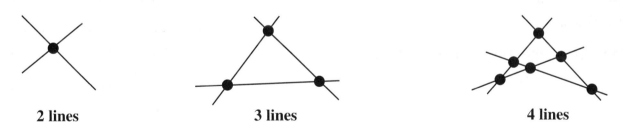

| **2 lines** | **3 lines** | **4 lines** |

An investigation like the one above immediately raises points for discussion, simply because it has been deliberately so poorly defined. What exactly does it mean? If it meant the fewest possible number of points of intersection, then the answer is always one, no matter how many lines there are. Are new lines allowed to go through intersections which already exist? If so, there are too many different answers to the question, depending on how the new line is drawn. The only sensible thing is to say that each new line must not pass through any previously existing intersection.

Once the rule is set, then the investigation can proceed and the answers can be seen on the second diagonal of Pascal's Triangle and in the table above.

What do you notice about the sequence of the number of internal regions in successive diagrams.

  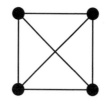 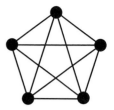

This problem is the dual of the previous one. Instead of counting the points where pairs of lines intersect, we count the lines joining pairs of points. The problem and its solution is essentially the same, but it is easier to establish the expression $n(n-1)/2$ as the means of generating triangle numbers. Each point (n) is joined to every other point (n-1), but this means that every line is counted twice, hence the need to halve the product. The diagrams above can be regarded as purely geometrical, but they can also be regarded as graphical representations of the "handshake" problem. Calculate the total number of handshakes if 2, 3, 4, 5, ... people each shake hands with everybody else.

If the "handshake" problem appears especially interesting to a particular group, then there are plenty of opportunities to promote further discussion. How many handshakes are there between all the people in a class, in a year or in a whole school? How long would it take to do this and how could it be organised?

SQUARE RINGS

It is curious that the product of the six numbers surrounding any element in Pascal's Triangle is always a perfect square.

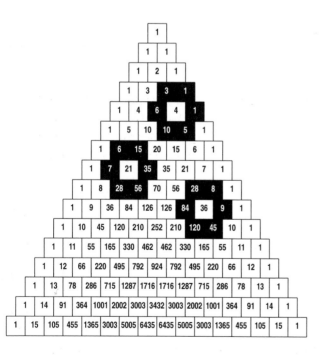

For example

$$1 \times 1 \times 5 \times 10 \times 6 \times 3 = 900 = 30^2$$

It is also true that the products of alternate triples are also equal.

$$1 \times 5 \times 6 = 1 \times 10 \times 3 = 30$$

Is it possible to find a connection between the number being surrounded and the value of the square?

TETRAHEDRAL NUMBERS

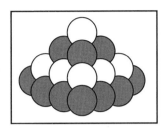

Just as it is possible to generate numbers called triangle numbers by adding extra rows to a triangle, it is possible to generate numbers called tetrahedral numbers by adding extra layers to a tetrahedron. This diagram shows a tetrahedron which has four layers, containing 20 (1 + 3 + 6 + 10) spheres. It is said therefore that 20 is the fourth tetrahedral number.

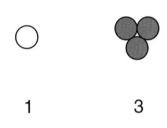  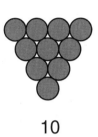

| 1 | 3 | 6 | 10 |

The number of spheres in each successive layer is a triangle number and the first four tetrahedral numbers are therefore

ONE LAYER:	1 = 1
TWO LAYERS:	1 + 3 = 4
THREE LAYERS:	1 + 3 + 6 = 10
FOUR LAYERS:	1 + 3 + 6 + 10 = 20

It will be observed that these numbers are the ones to be found on the third diagonal of Pascal's Triangle.

PYRAMID NUMBERS

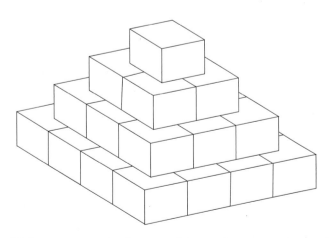

If a square pyramid is built of square layers of cubical blocks, then it is possible to generate another sequence of numbers which it might seem reasonable to call pyramid numbers.

ONE LAYER:	1 = 1
TWO LAYERS:	1 + 4 = 5
THREE LAYERS:	1 + 4 + 9 = 14
FOUR LAYERS:	1 + 4 + 9 + 16 = 30

This sequence of pyramid numbers are to be found in Pascal's Triangle by adding together the adjacent pairs of tetrahedral numbers on the third diagonal. This is the three-dimensional equivalent of adding adjacent pairs of triangle numbers on the second diagonal to get square numbers.

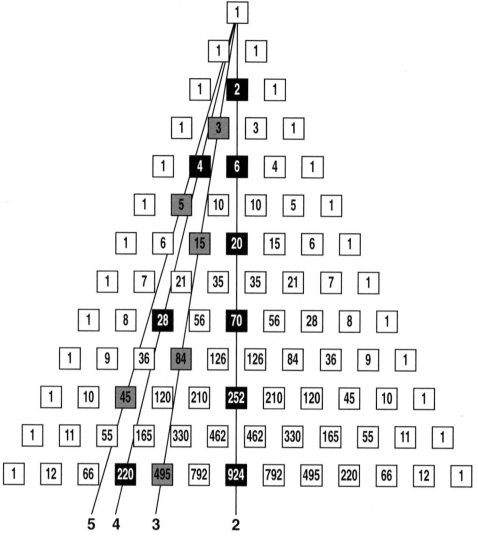

In all the blackline masters, the elements of Pascal's Triangle are each centred within their boxes, whether the boxes are visible or not. It therefore becomes possible to search for patterns of connections between numbers in the Triangle whose position are exactly co-linear. It makes a very interesting investigation to suggest this to a class.

It is very likely that at a very early stage someone will notice that all the numbers down the centre of the Triangle are even. They may also notice that those central even numbers occur in every second row.

Then suggest that they draw a line through the centre of 1 in row 0 and 3 in row 3. It is a fact that this line only passes precisely through certain numbers, starting with 15, 84, 495, 3003,.... One of these numbers occurs every third row and all of them divide by three.

Similarly there is a line starting at 1 which passes exactly through a number every fourth row and each of those numbers is a multiple of four.
A similar line is apparent for 5, 6, 7 ... etc.
Remarkable!

```
                      1

                   1     1

                1     2     1

             1     3     3     1

          1     4     6     4     1

       1     5    10    10     5     1

    1     6    15    20    15     6     1

 1     7    21    35    35    21     7     1

1     8    28    56    70    56    28     8     1

1     9    36    84   126   126    84    36     9     1
```

If the elements of Pascal's Triangle are printed or written without surrounding boxes, then it is easier to see each row as a single larger number. The elements are then regarded as digits within it.

Treated in this way, the sequence becomes

1, 11, 121, 1331, 14641, 15101051, ...

Once the first few rows are written like this someone is sure to notice that

$$1 = 11^0, \quad 11 = 11^1, \quad \text{and} \quad 121 = 11^2$$

Immediately suggest that they work out 11^3 and 11^4. Approached in the right way, this can be a most exciting discovery for a class to make.

Then suggest that they try 11^5. Since $11^5 = 161051$, they will not find it difficult to devise a simple carrying rule for obtaining it directly from the rows in Pascal's Triangle. The rule also works for 11^6, 11^7 and 11^8.

Row 9 is the first with elements with three digits.

1 9 36 84 126 126 84 36 9 1

Quite how far this idea is worth pursuing depends on the class but row 13 introduces the first number with four digits.

1 13 78 286 715 1287 1716 ...

This may also be a good time to introduce the Trachtenberg method of multiplying by 11.

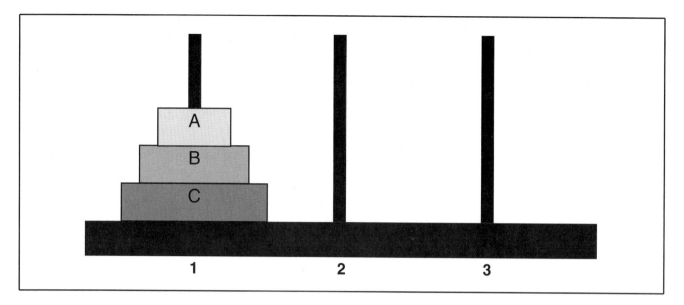

This is an interesting puzzle and it may originally have come from China or possibly even Hanoi! However, there is the strong possibility that it was invented by the American puzzle creator Sam Loyd. He may have pretended that it came from the Far East, in order to make it sound more mysterious. Whatever the truth of the matter, it is a puzzle which is liked by children over a wide age and ability range.

It consists of a set of discs, each with a hole drilled through its centre and arranged in order of size on one of three pegs. The illustration above shows three discs on peg 1. The aim of the puzzle is to move the pile of discs to another peg, transferring one disc at a time. The rules of the puzzle state that no disc can rest on one which is smaller than itself and the task is to complete the transfer in the fewest possible moves.

If we use the notation that moving disc A to peg 3 is represented by A3, then a solution of the puzzle can be written

$$\textbf{A3, B2, A2, C3, A1, B3, A3}$$

The transfer is therefore completed in a minimum of 7 moves.

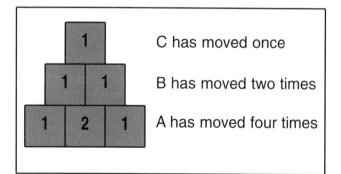

C has moved once

B has moved two times

A has moved four times

The first three rows of Pascal's Triangle show the pattern of moves.

$$1 + 2 + 4 = 7 = 2^3 - 1$$

With 4 discs, the total number of moves is $\qquad 1 + 2 + 4 + 8 = 15 = 2^4 - 1$

This puzzle is traditionally sold with 7 discs and so it takes $2^7 - 1 = 127$ moves to complete the transfer, assuming that no errors are made. Notice that each disc is moved twice as many times as the next larger and half as many times as the next smaller.

HEADS and TAILS

Any study of the properties of Pascal's Triangle, must inevitably include some work on probability. After all, it was in thinking about problems posed by gamblers, that Pascal originally discovered the Triangle. The best and simplest introduction to it is to consider coin tossing experiments. The probability of a "head" or a "tail" is exactly a half and experiments are easy to set up. Nor does it take too long to obtain some results. An important part of the value of this work is to learn to write down all the probabilities in a methodical way.

If three coins are tossed at one time or one coin is tossed three times, then the possibilities can be set out like this.

Possible result		Possible ways of obtaining this result	No. of ways	Probability
3 heads	0 tails	HHH	1	$\frac{1}{8}$
2 heads	1 tail	HHT HTH THH	3	$\frac{3}{8}$
1 head	2 tails	HTT THT TTH	3	$\frac{3}{8}$
0 heads	3 tails	TTT	1	$\frac{1}{8}$
			In total 8 ways	

With a sequence of 1,3,3,1 and a total of 8, there is clearly a connection with Pascal's Triangle.

The possibilities for 1,2,3 4, ... tosses of a coin can be set out in a similar way and then collected into a table, so that the connection with Pascal's Triangle is apparent to all.

	All heads	All heads except 1	All heads except 2	All heads except 3	All heads except 4
one coin	$\frac{1}{2}$	$\frac{1}{2}$			
two coins	$\frac{1}{4}$	$\frac{2}{4}$	$\frac{1}{4}$		
three coins	$\frac{1}{8}$	$\frac{3}{8}$	$\frac{3}{8}$	$\frac{1}{8}$	
four coins	$\frac{1}{16}$	$\frac{4}{16}$	$\frac{6}{16}$	$\frac{4}{16}$	$\frac{1}{16}$

Point for discussion

Is the probability of a baby being a boy or a girl exactly a half? In fact, the proportion is not 100 boys:100 girls as it would be if the probability were exactly 0.5, but 106 boys:100 girls. It is interesting to speculate why this might be and the apparent consequences for the balance of the population. This could be combined with collecting actual statistics within the school.

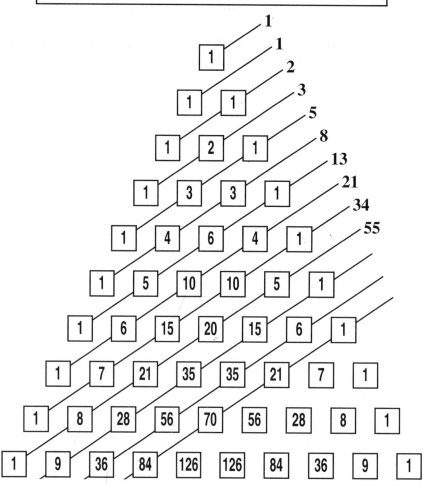

If the numbers of Pascal's Triangle are added together in the way suggested by the diagram above, then the following sequence emerges

1, 1, 2, 3, 5, 8, 13, 21, 34, 55, ...

Each number of the sequence is the sum of the previous two and so it continues for ever. They are called Fibonacci numbers after the Italian medieval mathematician who first proposed a problem about multiplying rabbits which generated the sequence. He did not study it in depth himself, but it has been observed that Fibonacci numbers occur in nature far more frequently than can be explained purely by co-incidence. If you have introduced investigations into the numbers which occur in pine cones, sunflowers, leaf shoots etc., then it is interesting to point out the connection with Pascal's Triangle.

Another interesting connection is with the "golden ratio" or "phi". This is the name given to the positive root of the quadratic equation

$$x^2 - x - 1 = 0$$

Phi is an irrational number and can be expressed in decimal form as

1.6180339887...

The ratio of successive members of the Fibonacci sequence above tends to become closer and closer to the golden ratio as the sequence continues.

CLIMBING STAIRS

Many modern houses have staircases with 13 steps. In how many different ways is it possible to run up a staircase taking either one step or two steps at a time?

This is a good investigation for use in class because it seems quite simple and straight - forward at first. Only when the work is under way does it emerge just how hard it is to keep track of all the possibilities. Even if coloured pencils or felt-tip pens are used, the diagrams quickly become muddled and it soon becomes obvious that a logical method of listing and classifying is needed. As with so many problems of this type, it is best to start the investigation by considering the number of ways for a staircase with only one step, then for one with two steps, then three ... and so on.

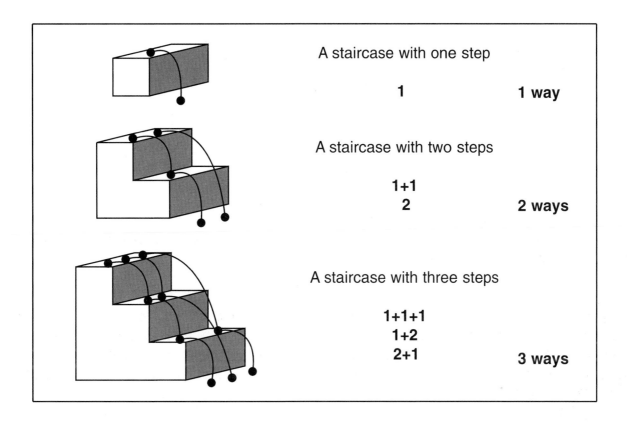

A staircase with one step

1   1 way

A staircase with two steps

1+1
2   2 ways

A staircase with three steps

1+1+1
1+2
2+1   3 ways

It soon looks as if this is a Fibonacci sequence and the class should be encouraged to search for shorter and shorter ways of listing the possibilities in order to be sure that it does indeed continue in the same way.

Once this is established, the answer to the problem can be seen to be 233.

The first fifteen Fibonacci numbers are

COUNTING NUMBERS	1	2	3	4	5	6	7	8	9	10	11	12	13	14	15
FIBONACCI NUMBERS	1	1	2	3	5	8	13	21	34	55	89	144	233	377	610

THE GARDEN PATH

You have twelve paving slabs, each two feet by one and have to make a path twelve feet long and two feet wide. How many different ways are there of laying the slabs?

This investigation is essentially the same as the previous one, but it could be introduced in a more practical way by asking the class to make twelve card rectangles each 2cm by 1cm or to make scale drawings of the completed path.

After a certain amount of practical work it is best to point out that a shorthand method is more appropriate if the aim is to enumerate the different possibilities. The illustration below shows the kind of approach which could be used.

	All vertical			Two horizontal			Four horizontal		Total
3 slabs	⏐⏐⏐			⏐ ═					
		①		═ ⏐	②				**3**
4 slabs	⏐⏐⏐⏐			⏐⏐ ═			═ ═		
				⏐ ═ ⏐					
		①		═ ⏐⏐	③			①	**5**
5 slabs	⏐⏐⏐⏐⏐			⏐⏐⏐ ═			⏐ ═ ═		
				⏐⏐ ═ ⏐			═ ⏐ ═		
				⏐ ═ ⏐⏐			═ ═ ⏐		
		①		═ ⏐⏐⏐	④			③	**8**

Once it becomes clear that a Fibonacci sequence is developing, then the solution to the problem proposed can be found from the list of Fibonacci numbers.
There are 144 different ways.

POSTAGE STAMPS

While sorting through the bottom drawer of her desk a secretary discovers a pile of 1p and 2p stamps. How many ways are there of arranging them on an envelope to make the value of a first class stamp

This is essentially the same problem again and its value lies in devising a methodical way of working.

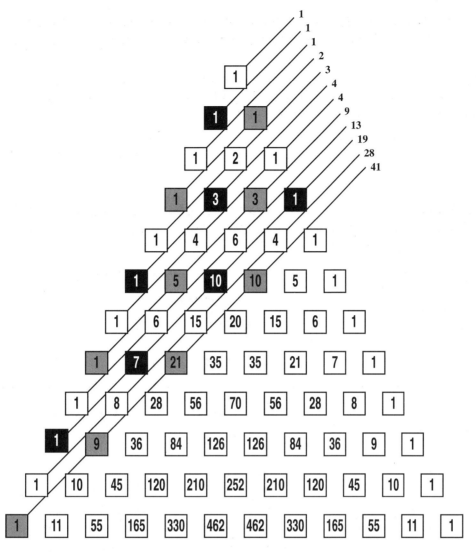

By increasing the slope of the parallel lines which gave the Fibonacci numbers, it is possible to generate another sequence which looks rather similar.

1, 1, 1, 2, 3, 4, 6, 9, 13, 19, ...

This time each number is the sum of three earlier consecutive numbers, but the answer is not written until after an interval of one number. For instance 1 + 1 + 1 = 3, and this 3 becomes the fifth term of the sequence. The ninth term 13 is obtained from the sum of 3 + 4 + 6, the fifth, sixth and seventh terms.

This same sequence of numbers can also be obtained from the investigations for stairs, slabs and stamps, but using 1 and 3 instead of 1 and 2 each time.

Although it is not so easy to see, it is possible to increase the steepness of the diagonal line still further and so generate yet another sequence.

1, 1, 1, 1, 2, 3, 4, 5, 7, 10, 14, 19, ...

In this case each number is the sum of four earlier consecutive numbers. The answer is written down after an interval of two spaces. For example 1 + 1 + 1 + 1 = 4, which becomes the seventh term of the sequence. The stairs, slabs and stamps investigations can be brought into service again, this time using 1 and 4 instead of 1 and 2.

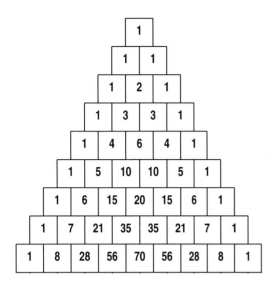

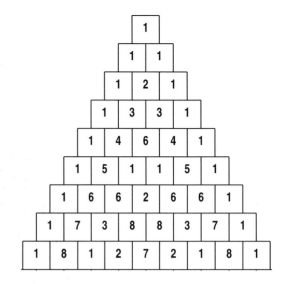

One problem with investigations into Pascal's Triangle is that the numbers at the centre become so much larger than the ones at the edges. For the first few rows it is possible to adjust the sizes of the handwriting or printing, but that soon becomes impracticable. An interesting and striking investigation which avoids this problem and which produces a whole range of new patterns is to work with digital roots. If each number is reduced to a single digit there is no difficulty in continuing the pattern for as far as is required.

For example:

The digital root of **21** is **2 + 1 = 3.**
The digital root of **84** is **8 + 4 = 12,** which in turn is **1 + 2 = 3.**
The digital root of **6435** is **6 + 4 + 3 + 5 = 17,** which in turn is **1 + 7 = 8.**

Note how the addition property is maintained in this manifestation of Pascal's Triangle Blackline Master 14 offers a useful outline for these investigations. Start by colouring the squares containing each of the nine digits in a colour of its own. What is the connection between the digital root and the remainder when the number is divided by 9?

Digital roots of square numbers

As a spin-off activity to this work it is interesting to consider what happens to the sequence of square numbers when they are reduced to their digital roots.

SQUARE NUMBERS	1	4	9	16	25	36	49	64	81	100	121	144	169	196	225
DIGITAL ROOTS	1	4	9	7	7	9	4	1	9	1	4	9	7	7	9

It is apparent that each third number is a nine and that the pattern

1, 4, 9, 7, 7, 9, 4, 1, 9

is repeated over and over again.

What happens to the sequence of triangle numbers when they are reduced to their digital roots?

The shaded areas show the pattern of those numbers whose digital root is 9. This means that the number in that position in Pascal's Triangle must be a multiple of 9.

(a) Rows 9, 18, 27, 36, 45 ... are mainly made up of nines. What would happen to the remaining rows of the triangle if one row could be entirely made up of nines?

(b) Why are 3 and 6 the only numbers which occur within the larger triangular outlines enclosing the smaller triangles of nines? Relate it to the diagram on page 8.

(c) Draw a graph showing the accumulating total or the proportion of nines as each new row is added to the Triangle.

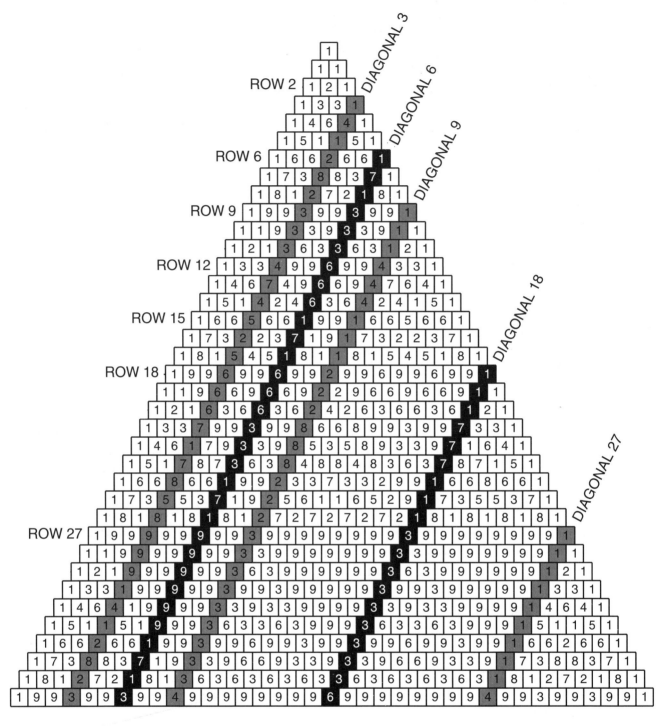

A more intensive investigation of the triangle of digital roots readily uncovers other patterns. On the page opposite some remarkable properties of rows and diagonals, which rather mysteriously seem to involve the number 3, are examined.

LOOKING for THREES

Patterns in rows

There seems to be a remarkable sequence of number patterns which occurs in rows whose row numbers form a geometric progression with ratio 3. For instance, in row 2 there is an element group (1, 2, 1). In row 6 it appears again, but separated by some sixes. In row 18 the group (1, 2, 1) can be seen once more but this time separated by some sixes and nines. Now the row numbers 2, 6, 18, ... form a geometric progression and it might be expected that the next row with this property should be 54. A check on a larger chart shows that the pattern is indeed maintained.

In row 3, the element group is (1, 3, 3, 1). This same sequence can also be seen in rows 9, 27 and 81, in each case separated entirely by nines.

A search for the element group (1, 4, 6, 4, 1) will find it on rows 4, 12, 36 ... in each case separated by threes and nines. A search for the element group (1, 5, 1, 1, 5, 1) will find it on rows 5, 15, 45 ... this time separated by sixes and nines.

If anyone can explain why this should be, we should like to hear from you!

Patterns in the diagonals

On diagonal 3 there is the sequence

1, 4, 1, 2, 8, 2, 3, 3, 3, 4 ...

On diagonal 9 there is the sequence

1, 1, 1, 4, 4, 4, 1, 1, 1, 2, 2, 2, 8, 8, 8 ...

On diagonal 27 there is the sequence

1, 1, 1, 1, 1, 1, 1, 1, 1, 4, 4, 4, 4, 4, 4, 4, 4, 4, 1, 1, 1, 1, 1, 1, 1, 1, 1, 2, 2, ...

There are also curious appearances of the multiplying factor three on the diagonals. An examination of diagonals

6, 18, 27, ...

shows a similar sequence of trebling, but neither of the sets of diagonals

2, 6, 18... or 4, 12, 36 ...

shows any such pattern. Anyone who is intrigued by such relationships might find it interesting to look at other groups of diagonals and see what rules can be constructed.

Natural or counting numbers

In the original version of Pascal's Triangle the first diagonal gives the counting numbers. In this digital roots version, the first diagonal becomes the digits

1, 2, 3, 4, 5, 6, 7, 8, 9, 1, 2, 3, 4, 5, 6, 7, 8, 9, 1, 2, 3, ... repeated endlessly.

These are the digits in modulo nine. They do not repeat again until diagonal 28, which is some 27 diagonals further on. Is it a total co-incidence that 27 is 3^3?

We looked at diagonal 3 in some detail, but did we notice that each third number gives the counting numbers again?

Perhaps we should stop this investigation here, for this way lies either enchantment or madness!

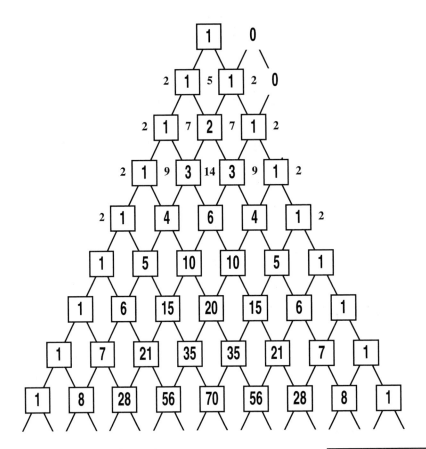

If all the diagonals are drawn in then they divide the Triangle into a lattice of rhombuses. A new pattern arises if the sum of the numbers at the four vertices are written within each rhombus.

```
    2  5  2
   2  7  7  2
  2  9 14  9  2
```

It immediately looks as if the normal addition rule for Pascal's Triangle applies and if you follow it for a few more rows, then it will soon become apparent that it does.

In this case the first diagonal does not list the counting numbers, but the odd numbers. Curiously this triangle does not seem to have a top as there is nothing which could sensibly be written for rows 1 or 0. However it has quite a number of patterns which are worthy of investigation.

(a) Add all the numbers in each row. $2 + 5 + 2 = 9$

(b) Add two to each number on the second diagonal.

(c) Add one to each number on the second diagonal and then write the number as a rectangle number. What pattern emerges?

(d) What happens if you regard each row as a number and then multiply it by 11?

Try generating similar rules using a lattice of equilateral triangles or a lattice of hexagons.

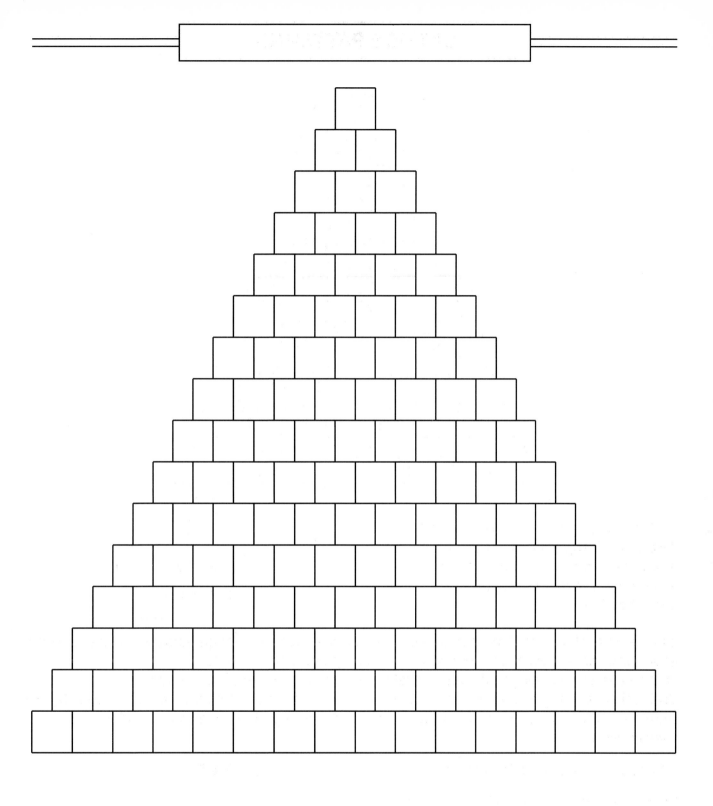

BLACKLINE MASTER 1

TARQUIN PUBLICATIONS

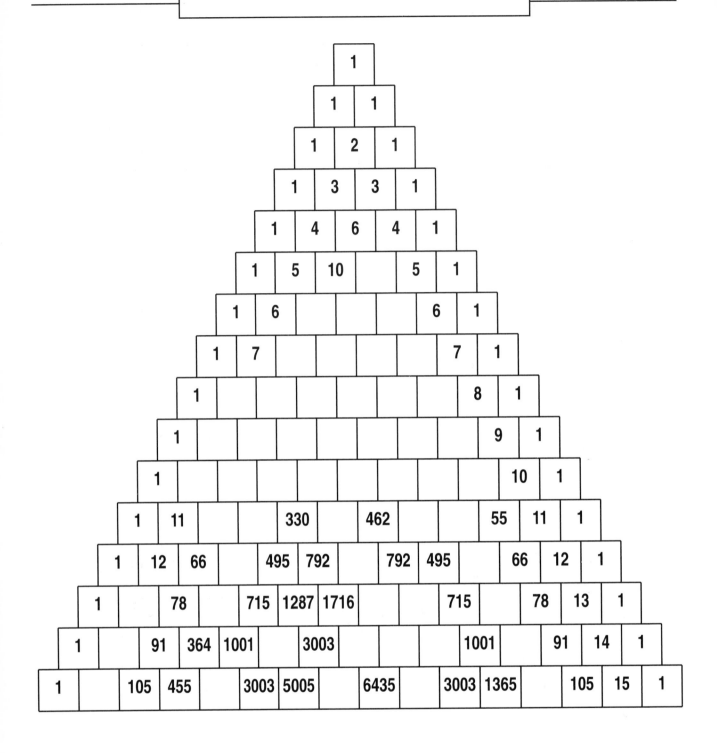

BLACKLINE MASTER 2

TARQUIN PUBLICATIONS

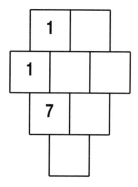

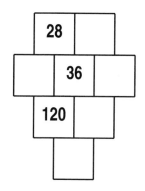

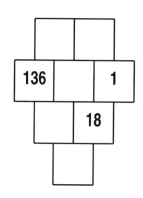

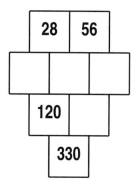

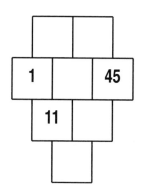

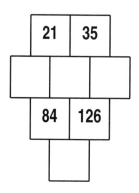

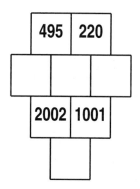

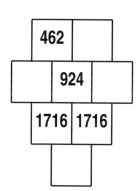

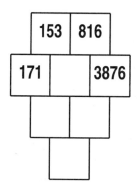

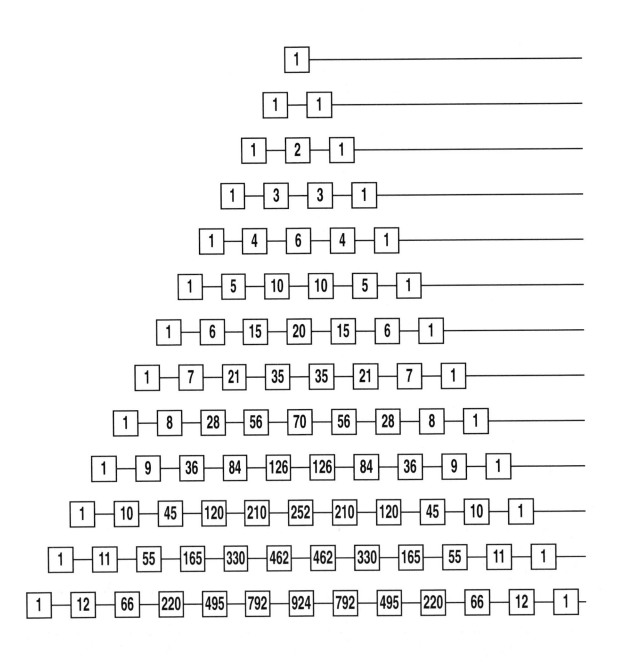

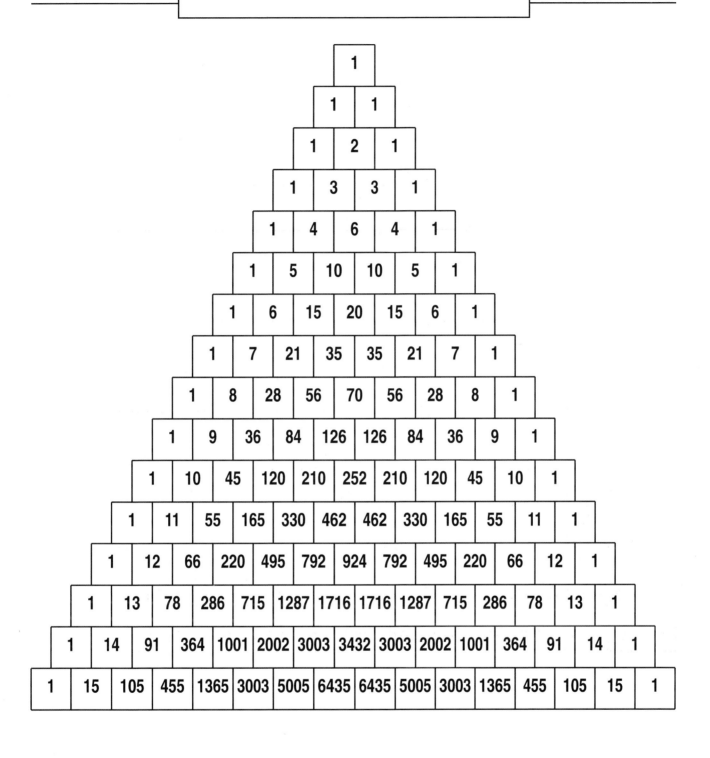

BLACKLINE MASTER 7

TARQUIN PUBLICATIONS

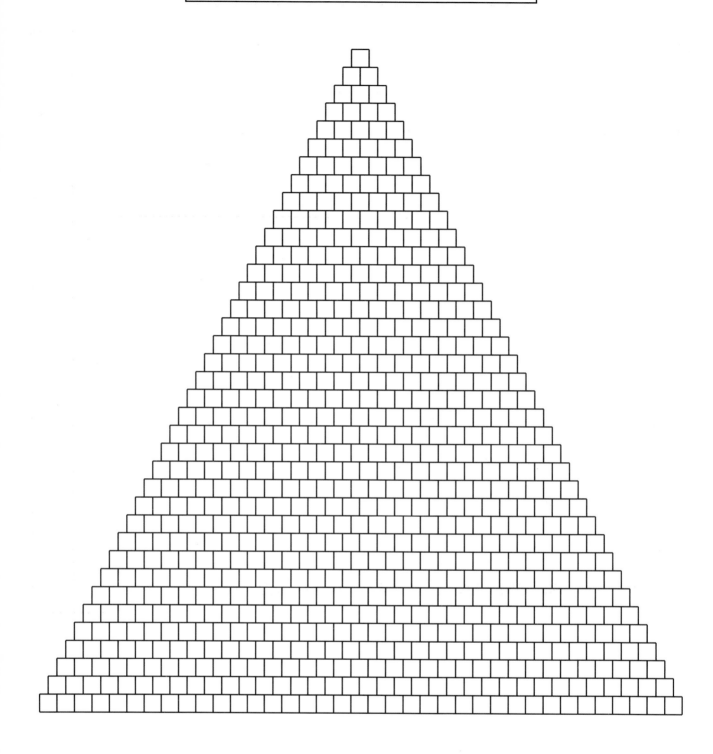

BLACKLINE MASTER 8

TARQUIN PUBLICATIONS

ROW

Row	Triangle values
0	1
1	1 1
2	1 2 1
3	1 3 3 1
4	1 4 6 4 1
5	1 5 10 10 5 1
6	1 6 15 20 15 6 1
7	1 7 21 35 35 21 7 1
8	1 8 28 56 70 56 28 8 1
9	1 9 36 84 126 126 84 36 9 1
10	1 10 45 120 210 252 210 120 45 10 1
11	1 11 55 165 330 462 462 330 165 55 11 1
12	1 12 66 220 495 792 924 792 495 220 66 12 1

```
                                    1

                              1           1

                          1         2         1

                      1         3         3         1

                  1         4         6         4         1

              1         5        10        10         5         1

          1         6        15        20        15         6         1

      1         7        21        35        35        21         7         1

  1         8        28        56        70        56        28         8         1

1         9        36        84       126       126        84        36         9         1

1        10        45       120       210       252       210       120        45        10         1

1        11        55       165       330       462       462       330       165        55        11         1

1        12        66       220       495       792       924       792       495       220        66        12         1
```

```
                              1

                           1     1

                        1     2     1

                     1     3     3     1

                  1     4     6     4     1

               1     5    10    10     5     1

            1     6    15    20    15     6     1

         1     7    21    35    35    21     7     1

      1     8    28    56    70    56    28     8     1

   1     9    36    84   126   126    84    36     9     1

1    10    45   120   210   252   210   120    45    10     1

1   11    55   165   330   462   462   330   165    55    11     1

1   12   66   220   495   792   924   792   495   220   66   12   1

1   13   78   286   715  1287  1716  1716  1287  715  286   78   13   1

1  14   91   364  1001  2002  3003  3432  3003  2002  1001  364   91   14   1

1  15  105  455  1365  3003  5005  6435  6435  5005  3003  1365  455  105  15  1
```

BLACKLINE MASTER 13

TARQUIN PUBLICATIONS

```
                                        1
                                       1 1
                                      1 2 1
                                     1 3 3 1
                                    1 4 6 4 1
                                   1 5 1 1 5 1
                                  1 6 6 2 6 6 1
                                 1 7 3 8 8 3 7 1
                                1 8 1 2 7 2 1 8 1
                               1 9 9 3 9 9 3 9 9 1
                              1 1 9 3 3 9 3 3 9 1 1
                             1 2 1 3 6 3 3 6 3 1 2 1
                            1 3 3 4 9 9 6 9 9 4 3 3 1
                           1 4 6 7 4 9 6 6 9 4 7 6 4 1
                          1 5 1 4 2 4 6 3 6 4 2 4 1 5 1
                         1 6 6 5 6 6 1 9 9 1 6 6 5 6 6 1
                        1 7 3 2 2 3 7 1 9 1 7 3 2 2 3 7 1
                       1 8 1 5 4 5 1 8 1 1 8 1 5 4 5 1 8 1
                      1 9 9 6 9 9 6 9 9 2 9 9 6 9 9 6 9 9 1
                     1 1 9 6 6 9 6 6 9 2 2 9 6 6 9 6 6 9 1 1
                    1 2 1 6 3 6 6 3 6 2 4 2 6 3 6 6 3 6 1 2 1
                   1 3 3 7 9 9 3 9 9 8 6 6 8 9 9 3 9 9 7 3 3 1
                  1 4 6 1 7 9 3 3 9 8 5 3 5 8 9 3 3 9 7 1 6 4 1
                 1 5 1 7 8 7 3 6 3 8 4 8 8 4 8 3 6 3 7 8 7 1 5 1
                1 6 6 8 6 6 1 9 9 2 3 3 7 3 3 2 9 9 1 6 6 8 6 6 1
               1 7 3 5 5 3 7 1 9 2 5 6 1 1 6 5 2 9 1 7 3 5 5 3 7 1
              1 8 1 8 1 8 1 8 1 2 7 2 7 2 7 2 7 2 1 8 1 8 1 8 1 8 1
             1 9 9 9 9 9 9 9 9 3 9 9 9 9 9 9 9 9 3 9 9 9 9 9 9 9 9 1
            1 1 9 9 9 9 9 9 9 3 3 9 9 9 9 9 9 9 9 3 3 9 9 9 9 9 9 1 1
           1 2 1 9 9 9 9 9 9 3 6 3 9 9 9 9 9 9 3 6 3 9 9 9 9 9 9 1 2 1
          1 3 3 1 9 9 9 9 9 3 9 9 3 9 9 9 9 9 3 9 9 3 9 9 9 9 9 1 3 3 1
         1 4 6 4 1 9 9 9 9 3 3 9 3 3 9 9 9 9 3 3 9 3 3 9 9 9 9 1 4 6 4 1
        1 5 1 1 5 1 9 9 9 3 6 3 3 6 3 9 9 9 3 6 3 3 6 3 9 9 9 1 5 1 1 5 1
       1 6 6 2 6 6 1 9 9 3 9 9 6 9 9 3 9 9 3 9 9 6 9 9 3 9 9 1 6 6 2 6 6 1
      1 7 3 8 8 3 7 1 9 3 3 9 6 6 9 3 3 9 3 3 9 6 6 9 3 3 9 1 7 3 8 8 3 7 1
     1 8 1 2 7 2 1 8 1 3 6 3 6 3 6 3 6 3 3 6 3 6 3 6 3 6 3 1 8 1 2 7 2 1 8 1
    1 9 9 3 9 9 3 9 9 4 9 9 9 9 9 9 9 9 6 9 9 9 9 9 9 9 9 4 9 9 3 9 9 3 9 9 1
```

BLACKLINE MASTER 14

TARQUIN PUBLICATIONS